FOOLS PARADISE
A Time For Separation?

U.S. Legal Fiction

(Previous edition of this book was under title Jesus vs. International Bankers)

Written By
Rasheed L. Muhammad

Acknowledgement

I thank the Great Mahdi of the Muslim world, Master W. Fard Muhammad, who came to North America to find and teach Elijah Muhammad. I thank Minister Louis Farrakhan for delivering his lecture series entitled, Jesus Saves to re-give the key to black America.

Lastly thanks to the author *of Understanding Your Name: the Straw Man* whose articles I employed throughout the pages of this book. Note: His articles were edited and revised versions of a work entitled "It's All in the Name", believed to be written by Michael Edward...trying to figure out why our name is written in ALL-CAPS, by looking through dictionaries, government regulations, and the like to see if it states anywhere what the purpose is?[1]

---

[1] http://fduniversity.wetpaint.com/page/Understanding+Your+Name%3A+the+Straw+Man

Table of Contents

PREFACE..7

CHAPTER 1 11

WORLD OF LEGAL FICTION 11

CHAPTER 2 21

FULL FAITH AND CREDIT CLAUSE......................21

CHAPTER 3 33

WHO OWNS A LEGAL PERSON 33
BANK LAW 40

CHAPTER 4 45

CAN WE INCORPORATE SELF 45
RENDER TO GOD A NATION 50

CHAPTER 5 53

BLACKS AND INDIANS...53
THE CHURCH..58
JESUS OPPOSED USURY 59
GOLD AND SILVER IN BIBLE PROPHECY 61

CHAPTER 6 65

LAND OF MAKE BELIEVE AND DEBT 65
UNITED STATES DECLARED BANKRUPTCY 68
MARK OF WHITE AUTHORITY 70

CHAPTER 7 73

FINAL CALL 73

Preface

The life and history of Jesus born 2000 years ago and raised in Egypt—land of former slaves and slave master—was retold 300 years after he was departed from among mankind. He was stealthily born in Palestine. His mother was a black woman named Mary (Maryam in Arabic).

Jesus (Isa in Arabic) was rejected by Roman authority for teaching pagans gentiles how to be free, justified, equal, clean and upright. One of the greatest secrets not retold about him is Jesus was a black man of peace (Islam) with curly hair.

Although the Islamic book, Holy Quran, mentions Jesus escaping a death plot and that upon his return, his community will be exalted above all other communities at the end of the world, ironically millions upon millions of Muslims talk very little about this aspect of Jesus of the Holy Quran. Why is the question?

Is it because the prophetic or future Islamic Jesus was to return in North America—land of former slaves and slave masters? Is it because Black people are the community of Jesus? Is it because this once lost people appear to be yet the most rejected and despised below income community? Is it because they are still so blind, deaf, dumb and fearful of white authority that they do not realize who they are nor how they will be exalted as the head of the new and not the old? What is white authority? It is the "law of necessity," under 12 USC 95. So how do we get to real freedom?

According the last Islamic prophet, Mohammed Ibn Abdullah, Jesus' return establishes a new government where wealth will be in abundance for all, and people will not pay taxes.

Under the current failing world order ruled under white authority via private central banking corporations, we all pay taxes to repay compounding interest rates into their coffers. Therefore, it is adjacent to old world lending schemes that an Islamic Jesus and his community are given a sign and authority to replace the old with equity and financial justice. [Matt 21:12]

Of course, many people will find it difficult to accept an Islamic Jesus as Black Man because they have been indoctrinated with white America's explanation about Jesus as a Caucasian with straight hair. Nevertheless, we are now at the end of the old world of white lies and fairy tales about Jesus as retold by members of the Caucasian race and how it justified implementing central bank monetary policy—the root of all evil.

The old Jewish and old gentile world order is rooted in the color of law in which it is difficult to win. *Color of law* meaning: the appearance or semblance, without the substance, of legal right. They have misused power, possessed by virtue of state law and made possible only because wrongdoer is clothed with authority of state, is action taken under "color of law."[2] Subsequently, their old

---

[2] Black's Law Dictionary, Fifth Edition, page 241

world is passing away before our eyes. White authority is now facing a ***third world war*** if it does not correct how money is distributed or recycled and how interest rates are applied to lending credit.

Rasheed L. Muhammad
June 19, 2012

Chapter 1

World of Legal Fiction

Legal fiction "laws," such as the Reconstruction Acts and the implementation of the Lieber Code (Martial Law) were instituted by [Abraham] Lincoln soon thereafter and became the basis for the current "laws" in the US. Every purported "Act" in effect today is de facto, based on colorable fictitious entities created arbitrarily, out of nothing, without verification, lawful foundation, or lawful due process. All of such "laws" are not law, but rules of rulership by force/conquest, originating from and existing in military, martial law

Every President of the United States since Lincoln [including Presidents Bill Clinton, George W. Bush and Barak H. Obama] has functioned by Executive Orders issued from a military, martial law jurisdiction with the only "law" being the "law of necessity," i.e. the War Powers. The War Powers are nothing new.

Lincoln's second Executive Order of April 1861 called Congress back into session days later, but not under the lawful authority, or lawful due process, of the Constitution. Solely in his capacity as Commander-in-Chief of the U.S. Military, Lincoln called Congress into session under authority of Martial Law.

<u>Since April of 1861, "Congress" has not met based on lawful due process.</u> However benevolent, every person in the United States lives under martial law as a legal person.[3]

Thus the reason America's African slaves were emancipated, not set totally free nor made citizens. Emancipated means: The act or process by which a

---

[3] http://fduniversity.wetpaint.com/page/Understanding+Your+Name%3A+the+Straw+Man

person is liberated from the authority and control of another person. The term is primarily employed in regard to the release of a minor from the control of another (such as a parent).

With the case of African slaves in North America, The ***Emancipation Proclamation*** is an executive order issued by United States President Abraham Lincoln on January 1, 1863, during the American Civil War using his war powers. It proclaimed the freedom of slaves in the ten states then in rebellion, thus applying to 3.1 million of the 4 million slaves in the U.S. at that time...The Proclamation did not compensate the owners, did not itself outlaw slavery, and did not make the ex-slaves (called freedmen) citizens.[4]

In the mean time, the positive outcome, as far as the slaves were concerned is if it were not for Allah (God) working through Lincoln's sanity, America's brutal slave master system would have continued for who knows how long. Nevertheless, enslaving the lost members of the black nation is at the root reason why America was doomed the moment she accepted slavery. Her system of slavery is what leads financially wise international private bankers of Europe to ultimately overthrow the U.S. government and its people. Was it practically four hundred years of free human labor and wealth accumulation, which gave way to an entirely new private commercial corporate creature?

Subsequently, all people, black white, brown, red and yellow, now owe debt payments to a private corporate

---

[4] http://en.wikipedia.org/wiki/Emancipation_Proclamation

world of bankers designed on the grounds of legal fiction and white authority. Their legal processes of rulership is designed whereby all "common" people must support "a fictional legal world order" by paying interest rates, via taxes, into the private bank accounts of this world's money lending central bank apparatus. People are now dominated under commercial law and may be defined as a negotiable instrument or human capital according the former President Bill Clinton's Executive Order No. 13037:

COMMISSION TO STUDY CAPITAL BUDGETING

(b) The **appropriate definition** of capital for Federal budgeting, including: **use of capital for the Federal Government itself or the economy at large**; ownership by the Federal Government or some other entity; defense and nondefense capital; physical capital and intangible or **human capital**; distinctions among investments in and for current, future...[5]

This study is arising because "we the people" live in a world where banks are people too and customers at the same [damn] time. As it stands, "we" are already GENERAL PROVISIONS under the Uniform Commercial Code. You ask, what is a Uniform Commercial Code.

The **Uniform Commercial Code** (**UCC** or the Code), first published in 1952, is one of a number of uniform acts that have been promulgated in conjunction with efforts to harmonize the law of sales and other commercial transactions in all 50 states within the United States of America.

---

[5] http://clinton4.nara.gov/pcscb/eo13037.html

The UCC is the longest and most elaborate of the uniform acts. The Code has been a long-term, joint project of the National Conference of Commissioners on Uniform State Laws (NCCUSL) and the American Law Institute (ALI),[1] who began drafting its first version in 1942. Judge Herbert F. Goodrich was the Chairman of the Editorial Board of the original 1952 edition,[2] and the Code itself was drafted by some of the top legal scholars in the United States, including Karl N. Llewellyn, William A. Schnader, Soia Mentschikoff, and Grant Gilmore.

The Code, as the product of private organizations, is not itself the law, but only a recommendation of the laws that should be adopted in the states. Once enacted by a state, the UCC is codified into the state's code of statutes.[6]

This code is a means though which the actual ruling bank families ("person" or organization) speak to those whom they rule. To become a The President or The Governor or a member of a state body politic means obey them or loss your political seat and possibly or job. Its no wonder the bible reads [Psalm 58:1-3], *"Do you rulers indeed speak justly? Do you judge uprightly among men? No, in your heart you devise injustice, and your hands mete out violence on the earth. Even from birth the wicked go astray from the womb they are wayward and speak lies."*

Little do people know, in legal terms, a bank (corporation) means: person—an artificial person— who has been given more rights to exist than a legal person. Well, what is a legal person?

It is one of the terms used predominantly by the present civil governments and courts in the United States.

---

[6] http://en.wikipedia.org/wiki/Uniform_Commercial_Code

[A] Legal person: a body of persons or an entity (as a corporation) considered as having many of the rights and responsibilities of a natural person and especially the capacity to sue and be sued. Merriam-Webster's Dictionary of Law 1996.

Person. I. A human being (a "natural" person).

2. A corporation (an ***"artificial" person***). Corporations are treated as persons in many legal situations. Also, the word "person" includes corporations in most definitions in this dictionary.

Old world religious leadership failed long ago to rightly govern over a natural person—human beings. Therefore, corporate law leadership has trumped Gods law with commercial law to rule the daily civil lives of human beings. Absurdly, today we have been reclassified as a legal person. All legal persons today are ruled or governed under corporate legal processes due to Section 28 United States Code (USC) § 3002. I demonstrate this point from codes 14 and 15 where it announces the following:

(14) "State" means any of the several States, the District of Columbia, the Commonwealth of Puerto Rico, the Commonwealth of the Northern Marianas, or any territory or possession of the United States.
(15) "United States" means—
(A) **a Federal corporation**;
(B) an agency, department, commission, board, or other entity of the United States; or
(C) an instrumentality of the United States.[7]

---

[7] http://www.law.cornell.edu/uscode/text/28/3002

It is very clear to the wide awake man and woman that **Section 28 United States Code (USC) § 3002 means** [*what may have been once upon a time called America is now*] **the "United States" a federal corporation**; also, referred to as: an agency, department, commission board and an instrumentality. The question is: an instrumentality of who and what?

Of course, most common people believe they exist under God's law of creation. The issue is do you or can you function and have a quality of life residing outside the world of legal fiction or legal processes enforced by the courts of the "United States" a federal corporation? About now, it will be too rough in a world without concrete, electricity and steel. So what is legal fiction?

The authors of *The Real Life Dictionary of the Law*, Gerald and Kathleen Hill, are accomplished scholars and writers. Gerald Hill is an experienced attorney, judge, and law instructor. Here is how the term legal fiction is described:

"Legal fiction. n. A presumption of fact assumed by a court for convenience, consistency or to achieve justice. There is an old adage: Fictions arise from the law, and not law from fictions." [8]

Here again, let's see how Section 28 United States Code (USC) § 3002 defines the word court. It reads:

(2) "Court" means any court created by the Congress of the United States, **excluding the United States Tax Court**.

---

[8] http://fduniversity.wetpaint.com/page/Understanding+Your+Name%3A+the+Straw+Man

USC code 3002 provides for the Congress of the United States to create any court, except a TAX COURT. Why not a tax court?

Is Congress complicit in an illegal or questionable act opposed to the main principle Jesus comes to establish i.e. free humanity from DEBT! Has Congress aided the enemies of the community of Jesus to subject human beings to the legal processes of an artificial corporate person via the "Court?" Does the U.S. Congress think it can hide God's law of economics, which they have temporary trumped by justifying a world of legal fiction to perpetuate white authority—the law of necessity?

Black Jesus of 2000 years ago was faced with similar powers, forces and political entities but none a greater force as we have with the "United States' a federal corporation and its Congress. The U.S. is ruled by modern money changers (international bankers) working in quasi-conjunction with Congress et al. So now we know what instrumentality the U.S. belongs. It belongs to an International bank given a legal fiction [person] status.

Jesus of 2000 years ago foresaw this type of diabolical system overtaking the wealth of the common people by fraud. He demonstrated his opposition against it by these words, [Matt 21:12] *"And Jesus entered into the temple of God, and cast out all them that sold and bought in the temple, and overthrew the tables of he money-changers, and the seats of them that sold the doves.* As one might conclude, 2000 years ago, a quasi-religious and Roman government bond to make ill gotten profits setoff Jesus to take corrective measures, on religious grounds, against finanical fraud. He openly opposed financial corruption.

Of course, our Black brother Jesus 2000 years ago was not against money-changers (bankers) for the sake of hating banking. He was against how they implemented their craft of banking or exchanging money to enslave people to debt as well as weakening the value of coinage. He understood how mishandling and mismanaging the means for exchanging goods and services devalued the common coinage of the people. He saw through the game played between government persons, religious persons calling themselves Jews and wealthy persons how local economies deteriorated and peoples spending power decreased.

Nowadays, real wealth is called commodities. As a result of financial fraud, at the highest levels of government, the end result means a small elite group of persons control all means of exchanging goods and services, thus enslaving or subjecting the masses to the whims of a devaluing paper dollar that make high taxes paid by the poor for commodities. Besides, devaluing common money (Federal Reserve Notes) via masses printing machines also causes enormous interest rates that are set upon the backs and labor of common people.

Soaring cost prices is no accident. High prices are calculated by very unjust circles of men and women living under a legal fiction status or an artificial person status known as a bank (corporation).

All member bank branches established in U.S. towns and cities fall under the Uniform Commercial Code

Article 1 – GENERAL PROVISIONS as a foreigner. Code (7) states:

"Branch" includes a separately incorporated foreign branch of a <u>bank</u>.

Why is a "BRANCH" of a bank a foreign corporation in the U.S.? For U.S. federal tax purposes, "foreign corporation" means a corporation which is not created or organized in the United States [9]

Was it fraudulent money changing (central banking policy authorized by government officials and Jewish Talmudic religious leaders) that Jesus opposed 2000 years ago? Like wise, will it also be his proverbial self-return, as a Muslim, who will oppose fraud at the highest levels of government during our day and time—the last days.

Tragically, today the "United States" a federal corporation is faced with a similar fraudulent money-changing scheme. Except today it's not manifested on Temple grounds in ancient Rome, it is manifesting on the grounds of the U.S. Federal Reserve Central Bank—a [person] and customer of the U.S. tax payer.

---

[9] http://en.wikipedia.org/wiki/Foreign_corporation

Chapter 2
Full Faith and Credit Clause

Today's commercial world is controlled by a small circle of men and women who's banking corporate apparatus prints money to lend to entire governments. This group owns all world central banks in one way or another. Its actual headquarter bank is located in Switzerland i.e., Bank of International Settlements (BIS)

> The mission of the Bank for International Settlements (BIS) is to serve central banks in their pursuit of monetary and financial stability, to foster international cooperation in those areas and to act as a bank for central banks. [10]

Up to this day, the "United States' a federal corporation has yet to repay what it has borrowed either due to compounding interest rates and/or financial illiteracy.

Today's powerful private banking families and individuals rule inside the "U.S." as a person based upon GENERAL PROVISIONS Article 1 of the Uniform Commercial code, which says under definition 4:

"**Bank**" means any person engaged in the business of Banking. [11]

In addition, it is their money we spend, money in which the U.S. government has adopted according Uniform Commercial code (24)

"**Money**" means a medium of exchange currently authorized or adopted by a domestic or foreign government. The term includes a monetary unit of account

---

[10] http://www.bis.org/
[11] http://www.law.cornell.edu/ucc/1/1-201.html

established by an intergovernmental organization or by agreement between two or more countries.

I hope the fiction is unraveled in that through a "bank" [person] is how the actual rulers rule over the "United States" a federal corporation, which in turn governs all legal persons residing in those states via its statutes. Why statutes?

These statutes are designed to deal with legal persons as individual consumers under Article 1 of the Uniform Commercial Code 11, which says:

Consumer" means an individual who enters into a transaction primarily for personal, family, or household purposes.

Notice how "consumer' means and individual. Why use the language of legal fiction to describe a man or women buying products as a consumer? Why are we defined as an individual in this case, but as a legal person in other cases? What is white authority hiding concerning their world of debt and slavery?

Essentially, the U.S. constitution is almost dead were it not for a few white Moslem Sons of good faith, because *lawful matters* are ethically enjoined in the law of the land—the law of the people—and are actual in nature, <u>not</u> implied, [such as it is in the world of legal fiction carried out in U.S. courts.] This is why whatever true law was upheld by the organic Constitution has no bearing or authority in the present day legal courts.[12]

---

[12] http://fduniversity.wetpaint.com/page/Understanding+Your+Name%3A+the+Straw+Man

In reality, the community of Jesus has lived among a criminal people whose constant criminal actions have maintained white authority in the Western Hemisphere. This world was built upon the necessity of law so those whom have been victims of their crimes, in terms of losing sovereign rights, have no recourse in any court unless someone is made master of the law.

So I ask who really owns a person in the "United States" a federal corporation and how do we get free? To discover who owns a "person", just ask your local judge. One might provide a statutory interpretation, meaning:

> Statutory interpretation is the process by which courts interpret and apply legislation. Some amount of interpretation is always necessary when a case involves a statute. Sometimes the words of a statute have a plain and straightforward meaning. But in many cases, there is some ambiguity or vagueness in the words of the statute that must be resolved by the judge. To find the meanings of statutes, judges use various tools and methods of statutory interpretation, including traditional canons of statutory interpretation, legislative history, and purpose. In common law jurisdictions, the judiciary may apply rules of statutory interpretation to legislation enacted by the legislature or to delegated legislation such as administrative agency regulations.[13]

In the "United States' a federal corporation, before any human being can gain a legal status to enjoy her commercial goods and services financed by bank credit, one must become a legal person under the legal processes of legal fiction. In other words, consent to be legally indebted to the central bank [i.e. person] apparatus of this

---

[13] http://en.wikipedia.org/wiki/Statutory_interpretation

world. They [central bank] are not merely any person, but "the person" who prints the money we spend everyday of the year. Now what is a person?

According to Webster's 1828 Dictionary, PERSON, noun. per'sn. [Latin persona; said to be compounded of per, through or by, and sonus, sound; a Latin word signifying primarily a mask used by actors on the stage.]

In U.S. courts, a person is also a legal fiction; otherwise, you do not exist and have no rights to justice. How does one become a legal fiction?

To become a legal fiction, you must be registered at the local Social Security Administration office by representing your birth certificate. Thereafter, you will receive a number on a social security card, which updates your status into a *fool's paradise* of legal fiction as a legal person. Afterwards, you can act out your life within the "United States" a federal corporation and pretend to be anyone you imagine real or imagined.

Without submitting birthrights to the Social Security Administration's legal process, you cannot buy or sell goods and services within the "United States" a federal corporation, as you might desire. [Rev 13: 16-17]

The Social Security Administration manages the Nation's social insurance program--consisting of retirement, survivors, and disability insurance programs--commonly known as Social Security; administers the Supplemental Security Income program for the aged, blind, and disabled; **assigns Social Security numbers to U.S. citizens; and maintains earnings records for workers under their Social Security numbers**.[14]

---

[14] Federal Register list

The U.S. courts created the Social Security Administration in 1936 for the sole purpose to keep track of and make a legal person to pay inordinate income taxes. But, isn't it interesting the Supreme Court of the U.S. once declared income taxes unconstitutional during the year 1894.

Income taxes evolved, but in 1894 the Supreme Court declared the Income Tax of 1894 unconstitutional in *Pollock v. Farmers' Loan & Trust Co.*. The federal government scrambled to raise money.

In 1906, with the election of President Theodore Roosevelt, and later his successor William Howard Taft, the United States saw a populist movement for tax reform. This movement culminated in February, 1913, with the ratification of the Sixteenth Amendment to the United States Constitution:

"The Congress shall have power to lay and collect taxes on incomes, from whatever source derived, without apportionment among the several States, and without regard to any census or enumeration."

This granted Congress the specific power to impose an income tax without regard to apportionment among the states by population. By February 1913, 36 states had ratified the change to the Constitution. It was further ratified by six more states by March. Of the 48 states at the time, 42 ratified it. Connecticut, Rhode Island, and Utah rejected the amendment; Pennsylvania, Virginia, and Florida did not take up the issue.

A copy of the very first IRS 1040 form, dated 1913, can be found at the IRS website showing that only those with incomes of $3,000 (adjusted for inflation, the equivalent of $68,612 in 2011) or more were instructed to file.[15]

Notice that what $3000.00 dollars bought in 1913, it takes $68,612.00 plus to buy the same items today i.e., food, clothing, shelter and luxury items. Why? It is owed to financial fraud committed by modern day money-changers working lock-step with the "United States" a federal corporation, its agencies; including the U.S. Congress. Obviously this unholy alliance is allowed by the U.S. Supreme Court. The question is: what part has the community of Jesus played in this legal fiction. Whatever part played or not played, U.S. Rep. Randy Forbes stated on Tuesday, January 24, 2012 in a blog post on the following:

"The national debt is equal to $48,700 for every American or $128,300 for every U.S. household..."

Again, without a social security card and birth certificate, you are not a legal person in the "United States" a federal corporation. That is because after registering for U.S. credentials, all are duped into immediate debt to a privately owned central bank [person]. This fictional person [bank] is The Federal Reserve Bank and its private owners earn great profits as an artificial person under the status as a corporation. A corporate entity does not have a body, soul, and spirit like man has, but is a fictitious entity created for the purpose of making a profit. You might want to begin this unlawful act by revisiting the "The Full Faith and Credit Clause in Article IV,

---

[15] http://en.wikipedia.org/wiki/Internal_Revenue_Service

Section 1 of the United States Constitution. This clause addresses the duties that states within the United States have to respect the "public acts, records, and judicial proceedings of every other state."

In the court of law, you fight legal fiction with legal fiction.

According to the Supreme Court, there is a difference between the credit owed to laws (i.e. legislative measures and common law) as compared to the credit owed to judgments. Judgments are generally entitled to greater respect than laws, in other states. At present, it is widely agreed that this Clause of the Constitution has little impact on a court's choice of law decision, although this Clause of the Constitution was once interpreted differently. This clause was never intended to enforce by policy through U.S. Congress, a legal process to make people pay debts owed to the privately owned Federal Reserve Central Bank incurred by the "United States" a federal corporation.

Resistance from the U.S. FED Central Bank's legal processes is futile unless the community of Jesus know how to take a call to action toward a complete freedom and rebel. Think this over! On July 11, 2001, our current U.S. President, Barak H. Obama, made the following statement while citing The Full Faith and Credit clause.

THE PRESIDENT: Good morning, everybody. I want to give a quick update on what's happening with the debt negotiations, provide my perspective, and then I'm going to take a few questions.

As all of you know, I met with congressional leaders yesterday. We're going to be meeting again today, and we're going to meet every single day until we get this thing resolved.

The good news is that all the leaders continue to believe, rightly, that it is not acceptable for us not to raise the debt ceiling and to allow the U.S. government to default. We cannot threaten the United States' full faith and credit for the first time in our history.

We have agreed to a series of spending cuts that will make the government leaner, meaner, more effective, more efficient, and give taxpayers a greater bang for their buck. That includes defense spending. That includes health spending. It includes some programs that I like very much, and we -- be nice to have, but that we can't afford right now.[16]

Okay, so the U.S. is in debt to private bankers and families around the world, including the Federal Reserve Bank for nearly 20 trillion or more dollars. Some figures calculate 100 trillion dollars. This accumulation of debt had been accruing since the 1930's. So now you know why your tax dollars are confiscated before receiving a paycheck. Bills must be paid in the name of legal debts and these debts or judgments are held against you and I?

How did 'we the people" get caught up in a "United States" a federal corporation debt debacle? Step 1: We became a registrant legal person upon receiving a social security card at the local social security office. Without this card, you are not positioned to repay upon the "United States" a federal corporations debt. So what is a legal person again? Are we fictional "alter ego" versions of a name, manufactured under the legal fiction of "right

---

[16] http://www.whitehouse.gov/the-press-office/2011/07/11/press-conference-president

of presumption" for purposes of jurisprudence? And is this legal or lawful?

As [A] legal person: a body of persons or an entity (as a corporation) considered as having many of the rights and responsibilities of a natural person, we do have especially the capacity to sue and be sued.

Since "we the people" can be sued and sue, can we sue the "United States" a federal corporation as body of persons or an entity to get relief from beneath U.S. corporate debt debacle?

To initiate a lawful suit might mean to retain those whom are degreed in merchant law, maritime law, constitutional law, common law, religious law and uniform commercial codes since this realm is from where legal fiction has been derived. Is this a suit that an organized entity can justify? Of course, since, "we" as a legal person reside in a corporation that has mismanaged its money to which it expects "us' to repay. Therefore, a lawful suit is in order now and here on behalf of the community of Jesus—as a body of persons or an entity. There is nothing to loss except mounds of debt. As Moses said to Pharaoh, "Let My People Go"! Was Moses indicating to a lawful suit? And can such a suit lead to a lawful separation between two nations of people, black and white?

A lawful suit entails the right is actful in substance that moral quality is secured. This lawful suit will be of biblical proportions to remove all legal processes and legal fiction hidden from consumers, by those whom have exploited us commercially. Perhaps this stands the reason why the bible reads in [Deuteronomy 1:16-17] "*I charged your judges at that time: Hear the disputes between your brothers and judge fairly, whether the case is between brother Israelites or between one of them and an alien. Does not show partiality in judging hear both small and great alike. Do not be afraid of any man, for judgment belongs to God. Bring me any case too hard for you, and I will hear it."*

Chapter 3
Who Owns A Legal Person

How did America lose its economic freedom? In 1913, the stage was set for the "United States" a federal corporation to be created by a greedy corrupt group of financial wizards. These private bank persons were legalized into artificial persons (corporate entity) as well. Now, 99 years later, they own all legal persons residing within the "United States" a federal corporation because we are in debt to a system they designed and imposed on the poor and ignorant U.S. Congress, December 23, 1913.

The most terrifying agency created by those financial wizards, in 1913, is the IRS—the collection agency affiliated with the privately owned and operated Federal Reserve Central Bank. I reiterate, this bank [person] receives profits from working class tax payers for merely being <u>berthed</u> within the "United States" a federal corporation. In fact, if "we the people" refuse to repay taxes, after receiving the money created by the Federal Reserve Central Bank, lent to the U.S. Treasury Department, imprisonment lies before us. Can U.S. Congress legally explain what part of "The Full Faith and Credit Clause" is this!

Now don't you want to know who owns the Federal Reserve Bank? According the Federal Reserve Board of Governors:

> As the nation's central bank, the Federal Reserve derives its authority from the Congress of the United States. It is considered an independent central bank because its monetary policy decisions do not have to be approved by the President or anyone else in the executive or legislative branches of government, it does not receive funding appropriated by the

Congress, and the terms of the members of the Board of Governors span multiple presidential and congressional terms.

Therefore, the Federal Reserve can be more accurately described as "independent within the government" rather than "independent of government."

The 12 regional Federal Reserve Banks, which were established by the Congress as the operating arms of the nation's central banking system, are organized similarly or corporations[17] to private corporations--possibly leading to some confusion about "ownership." [18]

With this information, might common people also own some its stock? In this world ruled by an artificial person [bank] via legal processes, as long as it is present, shareholder ownership must be allowed. All legal persons residing the "United States" a federal corporation must also benefit from the debt rather than merely repay a compounding debt that can never get repaid.

I repeat, can and should common people have access to own stock in the Federal Reserve Bank that lends money to the "United States" a corporation? Of course, all it takes is an act of Congress, members of the Federal Reserve Board and its secret private owners to approve the deal. Remember, this world is all Legal Fiction—legal processes formulated by mankind i.e. white legislators. By the power of the pin, common people can become shareholders of the U.S.'s central bank. This residual income will serve all very well.

---

[17] http://www.projectworldawareness.com/2011/07/chart-of-who-owns-the-federal-reserve-once-again/

[18] http://www.federalreserve.gov/faqs/about_14986.htm

For example, the Reserve Banks issue shares of stock to member banks. However, owning Reserve Bank stock is quite different from owning stock in a private company. The Reserve Banks are not operated for profit, and ownership of a certain amount of stock is, by law, a condition of membership in the System. The stock may not be sold, traded, or pledged as security for a loan; dividends are, by law, 6 percent per year. [19]

One of the few early charts naming the founding owners of the Federal Reserve Bank can be read below. Examination of the chart in the U.S. House Banking Committee Staff Report of August, 1976 has changed much today. However, the ownership is still dominated by bloodlines and family bonds under many different names and corporate entities.

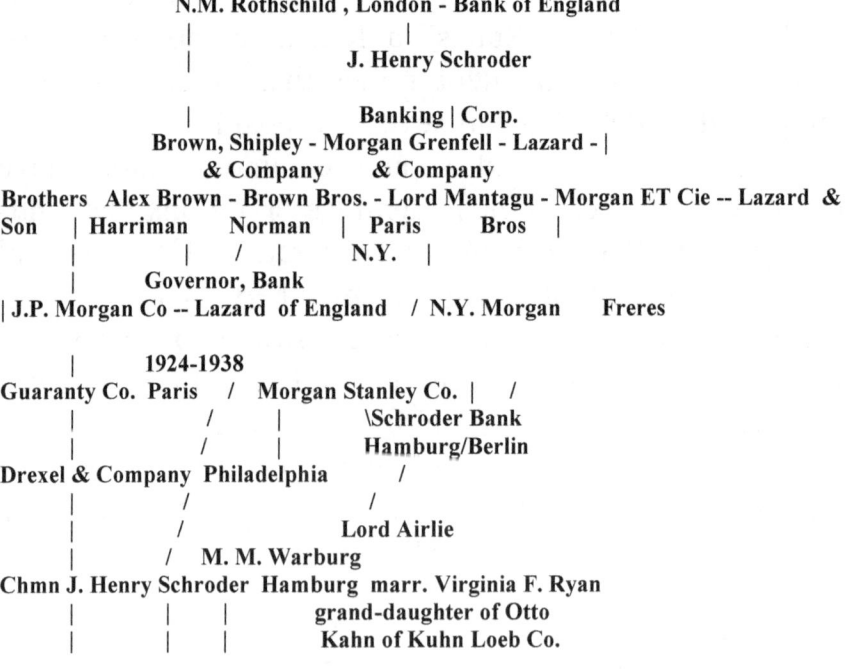

```
           N.M. Rothschild , London - Bank of England
             |                    |
             |              J. Henry Schroder

             |                Banking | Corp.
        Brown, Shipley - Morgan Grenfell - Lazard - |
             & Company        & Company
Brothers   Alex Brown - Brown Bros. - Lord Mantagu - Morgan ET Cie -- Lazard  &
Son   | Harriman     Norman   |  Paris       Bros   |
      |           |    /    |       N.Y.   |
      |          Governor, Bank
| J.P. Morgan Co -- Lazard  of England   / N.Y. Morgan      Freres

      |        1924-1938
Guaranty Co.  Paris    /   Morgan Stanley Co.  |   /
      |            /    |        \Schroder Bank
      |            /    |        Hamburg/Berlin
Drexel & Company  Philadelphia        /
      |        /                /
      |      /               Lord Airlie
      |    /   M. M. Warburg
Chmn J. Henry Schroder  Hamburg  marr. Virginia F. Ryan
      |       |   |           grand-daughter of Otto
      |       |   |           Kahn of Kuhn Loeb Co.
```

[19] http://www.federalreserve.gov/faqs/about_14986.htm

```
         |        |      |
Lehman Brothers N.Y --------------
Kuhn Loeb Co. N. Y.
Lehman Brothers - Mont. Alabama   Solomon Loeb
Abraham Kuhn
Lehman-Stern, New Orleans   Jacob Schiff/Theresa Loeb  Nina Loeb
Paul Warburg
Mortimer Schiff     James Paul Warburg
Mayer Lehman |    Emmanuel Lehman   \
Herbert Lehman    Irving Lehman       \
Arthur Lehman \   Phillip Lehman    John Schiff/Edith Brevoort Baker
         /    |          Present Chairman Lehman Bros

Robert Owen Lehman    Kuhn Loeb - Granddaughter of George F. Baker
        |    /        |
        |   /         Lehman Bros Kuhn Loeb (1980)
        |  /          |
        | /           Thomas Fortune Ryan
        | |           |
    Federal Reserve Bank Of New York |
    ||||||||          |
    _____National City Bank N. Y.    |
    |    |            |
    | National Bank of Commerce N.Y ---|
    | Hanover National Bank N.Y.       \
    |   |            \
    | Chase National Bank N.Y.         \
    |                |
Shareholders - National City Bank - N.Y.  |
James Stillman              /
Elsie m. William Rockefeller     /
Isabel m.  Percy Rockefeller     /
William Rockefeller

Shareholders - National Bank of Commerce N. Y.
J. P. Morgan            -----------------------------------------------
M.T. Pyne               Equitable Life - J.P. Morgan
Percy Pyne              Mutual Life - J.P. Morgan
J.W. Sterling           H.P. Davison - J. P. Morgan
NY Trust/NY Edison        Mary W. Harriman
Shearman & Sterling      A.D. Jiullard - North British Merc. Insurance
|              Jacob Schiff
|              Thomas F. Ryan
|              Paul Warburg
|              Levi P. Morton - Guaranty Trust - J. P. Morgan
|
Shareholders - First National Bank of N.Y.
J.P. Morgan
```

George F. Baker
George F. Baker Jr.
Edith Brevoort Baker
US Congress - 1946-64

Presently, the Federal Reserve Bank is so intertwined into all global affairs; it must allow common people to buy bank shares, at an affordable market, fixed under the regulation to guarantee profits. The price range should not go beneath $1.00 dollars or above $5.00 dollars per 13 day moving average. For what is worth, it is the bank [person] from where the "United States" a federal corporation borrowers its money to remain in business that we the tax payers repay via our income earnings, consumer taxes, state, city and local taxes.

What I mean to say is here we are more than 2000 years from the time a black man named Jesus preached in Palestine and modern day money-changers of the Federal Reserve Bank and U.S. Congress have not configured how to enable common people to own shares in a central corporate bank structure that owns trillions in wealth gained from the peoples sweat equity. Should debt be recycled, of course! Fraud can be stopped.

What is fraudulent debt in a world created for legal fiction?

An assumed debt is valid unless proven otherwise. ("An unrebutted affidavit, claim, or charge stands as the truth in commerce.") This is in accord with the Uniform Commercial Code, valid in every State and made a part of the Statutes of each State.

A name written in all caps—resembling a proper name but grammatically not a proper name—is being held as a debtor for an assumed debt. Did you incur that debt? If so, how and when? Where are the contract of indebtedness you signed and your proof of default thereon? The Legalities of All-Capital-Letters Names.[20]

I advise everyone to look at how your Legal Fiction name appears on your driver's license and social security card. Why all capital letters? Who did this to you and I?

> We could go on for hundreds of pages citing the legal basis behind the creation and use of all-capital-letters names. In a nutshell, fabricated legal persons such as "STATE OF TEXAS" can be used to fabricate additional legal persons.

> Fictions arise from the law, not the law from fictions. Legal persons originate from any judicial/governmental actor that wishes to create them, regardless of whether he/she/it is empowered by law to do so. However, a law can never originate from a fictional foundation that doesn't exist. [21]

Under legal fiction, common people must have access to own shares in the Federal Reserve Bank!

Until Jesus returns as the Islamic world expected, human beings are all trapped and snared into a Legal Fiction or a matrix of debt, including the white race.

Imagine if you will how the community of Jesus might incorporate every person within its sphere to receive the same 300 or more tax benefits as an artificial corporation [person]. Then watch how wealth redistributes and creativity is shared.

Think for a moment, the Federal Reserve Bank [person] holds our common wealth; therefore, it must be here from where real wealth is truly redistributed and recycled to the people to eliminate all fraudulent debt.

---

[20] http://fduniversity.wetpaint.com/page/Understanding+Your+Name%3A+the+Straw+Man

[21] http://fduniversity.wetpaint.com/page/Understanding+Your+Name%3A+the+Straw+Man

Wealth redistribution makes practical sense when one understands how electronic currency works. After all, money is artificially created out of nothing but a machine. A machine made by men and women. Accordingly, the law of necessity must be outdated and updated for an instant new age, almost overnight.

Perhaps people should get together and try something different other than consenting to bank law. Why not seek shareholder ownership in the Federal Reserve Central Bank. See what happens. Have you ever ask yourself, what is Bank Law?

Bank Law

Many conspiracy theorists articulate that there are two different kinds of Law on the planet. The first is known as COMMON LAW, which is Law of the Land. The other is Maritime Admiralty, which is also known as the Law of Water; it can also be referred to as Banking Law.

Maritime Admiralty Law considers people a Maritime Admiralty Product simply because we were birthed out of our mother's bag of water. The question to pose is what is a berth (birth) under commercial law or Maritime Admiralty Law?

Birth (Berth) under maritime law means to pull into a dock at a wharf such as when a ship comes into a dock. So consequently, when a ship pulls into a port, it pulls in and stops, that is called its berth, because the ship has now arrived. And because it is on the laws of the high seas, it is governed by the UCC Commercial Law. So when the ship pulls in to its berth, the first thing the captain must do is to present a certificate of manifest to the port authorities. What is a certificate of manifest?

It is a document listing a ship's contents, cargo, crew, and passengers. So whatever the ship brings in at berth, the captain has to present a certificate of manifest showing the identity and value of the items on the ship.

Now consequently, when people are born, conspiracy theorists go on to say, they come out of their mother's water, therefore they must have a birth certificate, which is a certificate of manifest, because the people are considered products within the United States--a federal Corporation. This is why a U.S. birth certificate contains a file number to assure the central bank infrastructure earns a profit from tax payers within their world of legal fiction (a fool's paradise) governed via what is called Uniform Commercial Code. (See sample copy of actual birth certificate)

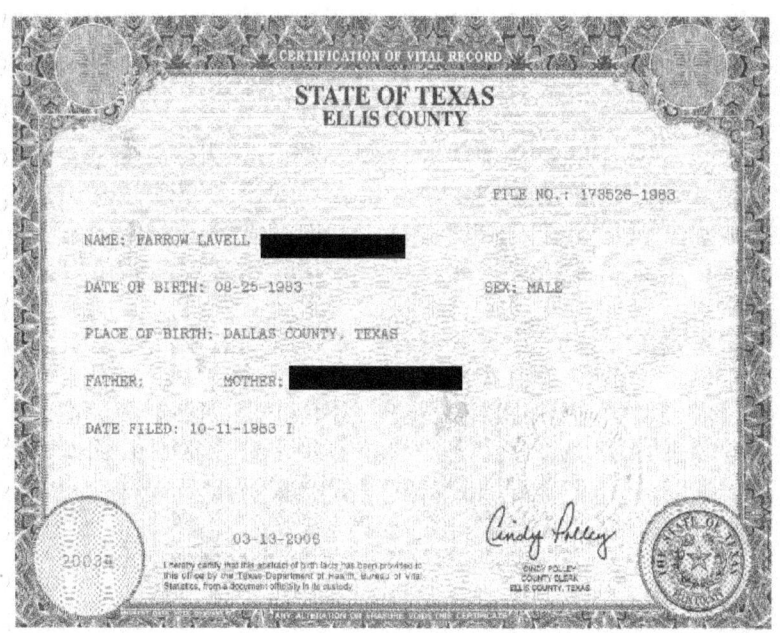

Before 1921 the records of births and names of children were entered into family bibles, as were the records of marriages and deaths. These records were readily accepted by both the family and the law as "official" records.

Since the U.S. went bankrupt in 1933, all new money has to be borrowed into existence. All states started issuing serial-numbered, certificated "warehouse receipts" for births and marriages in order to pledge the people as collateral against those loans and municipal bonds taken out with the Federal Reserve's banks.

"Full faith and credit" of the American people is said to be that which back the nation's debt. That simply means the American people's ability to labor and pay back that debt. In order to catalog its laborers, the government needed an efficient, methodical system of tracking its property to that end.

Humans today are looked upon merely as resources - "human resources," that is. Why do you think when you call to see if a company is hiring, you have to go through a division known as Human Resource?

The people are resources [human capital] to the government, their birth certificates are a security on the New York Stock Exchange, which is why if you look at all birth certificate's in America, it will say at the bottom this is printed on security paper, do not accept if not on full color security paper. At the bottom, you will always have a series of numbers, red numbers printed on the birth certificate, in which those numbers are a security stock exchange number on the World Stock Exchange, in which the American people are worth money to the International Bank that bought the government in the 1930's.[22]

A **conspiracy theory** explains an event as being the result of an alleged plot by a covert group or organization or, more broadly, the idea that important political, social or economic events are the products of secret plots that are largely unknown to the general public.[23]

Whether you believe or don't believe the above conspiracy theory put forth, you and I have been hoodwinked and bamboozled into debt to a private group of bankers and/or families (fool's paradise).

---

[22] http://www.macquirelatory.com/Birth%20Certificate%20Truth.htm

[23] http://en.wikipedia.org/wiki/Conspiracy_theory

Chapter 4

Can We Incorporate Self

I know this chapter deals with lawful and legal matters you might not comprehend. If this becomes the case, it stands the reason why the writers of legal fiction became gods of this world of legal fiction. God's law need not apply.

For instance, a corporation incorporated under de jure law, i.e. by bona fide express contract between real beings capable of contracting, is a legal fact.

Using the juristic artifice of "presumption," or "assumption" (a device known as a "legal fiction"), implied contract, constructive trusts, another entirely separate entity can be created using the name of the bona fide corporate legal fact (the name of the corporation) by altering the name of the corporation into some other corrupted format, such as ALL-CAPITAL LETTERS or abbreviated words in the name.

The corporation exists in law, but has arbitrarily been assigned another NAME. No such corporation (legal fact), nor any valid law, nor even a valid legal fiction, can be created under the "law of necessity," i.e. under "no law."

Likewise, the arbitrary use of the legal-fiction artifice of "right of presumption" (over unwary, uninformed, and usually blindly trusting people) can be legitimately exercised under "no law."

Anything whatsoever done under alleged authority of naked criminal aggression, i.e. law of necessity, can be rendered legitimate. Maxims of law describing "necessity" include: A person created under de jure law, with the person's identifying name appearing as prescribed by law and according to the rules of English grammar, is a legal fact. A fictional "alter ego" version of that name, manufactured under the legal fiction of "right of presumption" for purposes of jurisprudence. Is this legal or lawful.

It is crucial to define the difference between legal and lawful. The generic Constitution references genuine law. The present civil authorities and their courts use the word legal. Is there a difference in the meanings? The following is quoted from A Dictionary of Law 1893:

> *Lawful. In accordance with the law of the land; according to the law; permitted, sanctioned, or justified by law. "Lawful" properly implies a thing conformable to or enjoined by law; "Legal", a thing in the form or after the manner of law or binding by law. A writ or warrant issuing from any court, under color of law, is a "legal" process however defective. See legal. [Bold emphasis added]*
>
> *Legal. Latin legalis. Pertaining to the understanding, the exposition, the administration, the science and the practice of law: as, the legal profession, legal advice; legal blanks, newspaper. Implied or imputed in law. Opposed to actual*
>
> *"Legal" looks more to the letter [form/appearance], and "Lawful" to the spirit [substance/content], of the law.*
>
> *"Legal" is more appropriate for conformity to positive rules of law; "Lawful" for accord with ethical principle. "Legal" imports rather that the forms [appearances] of law are observed, that the proceeding is correct in method, that rules prescribed have been obeyed;*
> *"Lawful" that the right is actful in substance, that moral quality is secured.*
>
> *"Legal" is the antithesis of equitable, and the equivalent of constructive. 2. Abbott's Law Dic. 24. [Bold emphasis added]*

Legal matters administrate, conform to, and follow rules. They are equitable in nature and are implied (presumed) rather than actual (express). A legal process can be defective in law. This accords with the previous discussions of legal fictions and color of law.

To be <u>legal</u>, a matter does not follow the <u>law</u>. Instead, it conforms to and follows the rules or form of law. This may help you to understand why the Federal and State Rules of Civil and Criminal Procedure are cited in every court petition so as to conform to legal requirements of the specific juristic persons named, e.g., "STATE OF GEORGIA" or the "U.S. FEDERAL GOVERNMENT" that rule the courts.

Lawful matters are ethically enjoined in the law of the land—the law of the people—and are actual in nature, <u>not</u> implied. This is why whatever true law was upheld by the organic Constitution has no bearing or authority in the present day legal courts.[24]

It is impossible for anyone in "authority" today to access, or even take cognizance of, true law since "authority" is the "law of necessity," 12 USC 95. Hence, the term color of law is made evident. For this reason, the Islamic world has prophesized about the return of Jesus, as a Muslim. He has one foot on land and one foot on sea. More on this subject in chapter 5.

The entire concept of merchant, commercial or corporate legal processes used as a ""godhood" to trump God's law to govern men and women was instituted in North America on December 23, 1913. Although corporate or merchant legal processes were being utilized

---

[24] http://fduniversity.wetpaint.com/page/Understanding+Your+Name%3A+the+Straw+Man

during 16thcentury Europe, American Congressmen fully surrendered to its practice around 1933.

The question is: Will the "United States" a federal corporation and its central Federal Reserve Bank reform in time to do the work of Jesus as foretold by the Muslims? For instance, the last Islamic Prophet, Mohammed Ibn Abdullah said of Jesus' return:

> God's Messenger said: By him in whose hands my soul is, (Jesus) son of Mary will descend amongst you shortly as a just ruler and will break the cross and kill the pig and abolish taxes. **Wealth will flow (in such abundance that) nobody will accept (any charitable gifts).** (Bukhari 3/425, Muslim 1/p. 255).

Millions of Christians are unaware how they fulfilled, in 1936, their scripture where it reads, *"And he causeth all, both small and great, rich and poor, free and bond, to receive a mark in their right hand, or in their foreheads: and that no man might buy or sell, save he that had the mark, or the name of the beast, or the number of his name." Rev 13: 16-17.* I can only imagine how quick lawful freedom will be regained when Christians and the Muslim community of Jesus realize how a Representment claim to Congress might return our economies funds and stock back to its true functionality that is restore the wealth of the people.

Millions of Black Christians do not know Jesus and his community are only as alive as much as they make it alive as to fulfill the answer of his return. Nevertheless, the call to action is certainly decided in Islam's expression of freedom given by the last Muslim Prophet. He said what Jesus would do economically upon his return i.e., abolish taxes.

As it were, you'll read in both books (Bible and Quran) that heaven is nothing less than wealth upon wealth for everyone living and breathing. We live on earth, floating in the heavens. So why does debt rule the order of business on God's earth that is in heaven now and here?

Render To God A Nation

In conclusion, how does one render unto modern rulers/lenders what is theirs and to God His things? Go to the source of how legal procedures are written through U.S. legislators whom all proclaim to be Christians or Shriners (white Moslem son) or Jews. Then ask them to rewrite lawful means by which the community of Jesus will be free from debt on this earth here and now. Then see what happens. If the people want their wealth returned as a God given birthright, call for Islamic economic principles to be lawfully written and leave alone religious stories and exegesis.

Heaven on earth is Money, Good Homes, Luxury and Friendships in all occupations.

There are many ways to cause wealth and capital to accumulate. You can invest capital (or time and labor) directly in some endeavor, such as a business, which involves both risk and work. Or, you can lend money out at interest, requiring collateral to eliminate risk, and charge interest, which involves no work. Obviously, the second way is easier, and it is dishonest because it involves no risk and no work. Contrary to popular thought, forbidding loans at interest would not destroy an economy. Money would still be put to good use as people invest it directly into the economy. In fact, people would be more likely to invest in stocks (directly into the economy) if bonds were simply not available.

In fact, it is not even necessary to pass laws forbidding loans at interest, nor is it necessary to prosecute either borrowers or lenders for participating in such transactions. What is needed is for the government to simply not recognize contracts which charge interest as being valid contracts, just as any contract which is based on an illegal practice, combined with fraud and deception and lack of disclosure should not be valid. What this means is that lenders should not be able to demand that the government enforce payment or transfer of collateral when payment becomes impossible.

When you understand that those who loan money at interest will be able to enslave the people to whom they make loans, it helps to explain what is being described in Nehemiah Chapter 5.[25]

---

[25] http://www.bibleprophesy.org/goldsilver.htm

Chapter 5

Blacks and Indians

The Native American is the original inhabit of North America.

Under Authority: 20 U.S.C. 1401 (12 (13), Native Americans are referred to as Indian—

(a) Indian means an individual who is a member of an Indian tribe.

(b) Indian tribe means any Federal or State tribe, band, rancheria, pueblo, colony, or any Alaska Native village or regional village corporation (as established under the Alaska Native Claims Settlement Act, 43 U.S.C. 1601 et seq.)

(c) Nothing in this definition is intended to indicate that the Secretary of the Interior is required to provide services or funding to a State Indian tribe that is not listed in the Federal Register list of Indian entities recognized as eligible to receive services from the United States, published pursuant to Section 104 of the Federally Recognized Indian Tribe List Act of 1994, 25 U.S.C. 479a-1.

Notice how legal fiction works under "White" Authority i.e., Satan's rule a law. He defines Indian to mean an individual. What is an individual?

Individual as a noun, this term denotes a single person as distinguished from a group or class, and also, very commonly, a private or natural person as distinguished from a partnership, corporation, or association; but it is said that this restrictive signification is not necessarily inherent in the word, and that it may, in proper cases, include artificial persons.

> See Bank of U. S. v. State, 12 Smedes & M. (Miss.) 400; State v. Bell Telephone Co. 30 Ohio St. 310, 38 Am. Rep. 583; Pennsylvania it. Co. v. Canal Com'rs, 21 Pa. 20.

As an adjective, "individual" means pertaining or belonging to, or characteristic of, one single person, either in opposition to a firm, association, or corporation, or considered in his relation thereto.[26]

On the other hand, America's former slave descendents were defined a "person" sometime after the emancipation proclamation. So the choice given to the conquered Indian and to the former slave (both usually blindly trusting people), under white authority, is: Do you want to be seen as an individual or a person. Or are we and We BE ONE NATION—that is America's former slaves and Native Americans! Whereas the Native Americans' migrated to North America 16,000 years ago and the black man and women were kidnapped from Africa and enslaved in North America 457 years from today, both remain politically feeble and conduct business in a tribal approach thus remaining feeble under "white authority."

For instance, in 1871 the Indian Appropriations Act was passed to prevent those tribes from becoming an independent nation.

The Indian Appropriations Act of 1871 had two significant sections. First, the Act required the Federal Government no

---

[26] http://thelawdictionary.org/individual/

longer interact with the various tribes through treaties, but rather through statutes by stating, in part, "[n]o Indian nation or tribe within the territory of the United States shall be acknowledged or recognized as an independent nation.[27]

Thereafter, six years later in 1877 the U.S. Government *in the name of jim crow and black code laws* was instituted to prevent America's ex-slaves from constructing an independent nation after Abraham Lincoln's Emancipation Proclamation.

In the different states Reconstruction began and ended at different times; federal Reconstruction finally ended with the Compromise of 1877. Reconstruction policies were debated in the North when the war began, and commenced in earnest after the Emancipation Proclamation, issued on January 1, 1863…

This was followed by a period that white Southerners labeled Redemption, in which white-dominated state legislatures enacted Jim Crow laws and (after 1890) disenfranchised most blacks and many poor whites through a combination of constitutional amendments and electoral laws. The white Democrat Southerners' memory of Reconstruction played a major role in imposing the system of white supremacy and second-class citizenship for blacks, known as the age of Jim Crow.[28]

Of the two peoples, the Black nation and Red nation, the black man is most spiritually dead and is yet a legal captive in America. This is why the Honorable Elijah Muhammad taught:

---

[27] 25 U.S.C. § 71. Indian Appropriation Act of March 3, 1871, 16 Stat. 544, 566
[28] http://en.wikipedia.org/wiki/Reconstruction_era_of_the_United_States

The 18th verse of the 1st Chapter of the Revelation of St. John reads like this: *"I am he that liveth, and was dead; and, behold, I am alive for ever more,"* This does not refer now to the God, but refers to one of the mentally dead Negroes, who had been dead to the knowledge of truth and self and God -and now has been brought to life (Knowledge), and, has now been given authority over mental death in these words: "and have the keys of hell and of death.

The Keys mean authority and wisdom of how to execute the authority ....

"of hell" means the condition of the people of his, in hell, under a people who had killed them mentally.

This key he says, and I quote *"... and of death"* does not mean the natural, literal death that comes to everyone, but it means that this key of authority and enlightenment would destroy the death of ignorance and the mental death of the people of God, in hell. Not a burning, literal fiery hell, as the reader may think, but a hell of condition of life - being deprive of the essential things of life. [29]

Make no mistake about it. We are all residing under white authority on a mundane level. Their "authority" is the "law of necessity," under 12 USC 95. That's why the term "color of law" is justified under their rule of law.

By virtue of the word of God whose proper name is Allah, the Black and Red nations' have been scared by a hell-raising race (Jews and Gentiles) whose control over land and sea was hidden using legal fiction via merchant law. [Matt. 23:15] *"How terrible it will be for you, scribes and Pharisees, you hypocrites! You travel over land and sea to*

---

[29] http://www.muhammadspeaks.com/TrueHistoryJesus.html

make a single convert, and when this happens you make him twice as fit for hell as you are." By today's standards, modern Pharisees are no more than hhaughty and arrogant legalist. That is the worst Gentile conservatives of the conservatives—the fundamentalists of the fundamentalists, the neocons and Zionist.

The Church

During these modern times, the Church is relegated to function as an incorporate body[30] combined into one body or unit; united and organized as a legal corporation.

Think for a moment how Jesus' foes have become so powerful they have made religious proselytizing and its charity collection efforts only permissible under a 503(c)(3) federal tax-exempt status. By these legal procedures, what can the community of Jesus today establish unto God the things that are God's?

The bible story about Jesus 2000 years ago says he asked the people *"why do you put test to me about what belongs to Caesar?"* Then he said to one of the people, *"bring me a denarius (money) to look at...whose image and inscription is this?"* They said to him 'Caesar's'. Afterward, Jesus said, *'Pay back Caesar's things to Caesar, but God's things to God".* It doesn't get any clearer folks, paying back to God what is God's mean building a lawful God type-government with the funds Caesar provides to you after taxes.

---

[30] Corporations under 503(c) (3) federal tax-exempt status permit today in western civilization religious proselizing and money collection. All corporations are Juristic persons in Legal Fiction.

The Black and/or African American Christian clergy is so confused and fearful, they no not how to render to God, the things that are Gods. I ask, can the church establish a new governmental financial system, one that leads to freedom, justice, equality and wealth redistribution? If so, will Caesar et al remove the churches 503 (c)(3) status? If he does, then welcome to hell. (Smile) How else can an entity utilize the Federal Reserve Central Bank to make use of it to benefit God's thing? Answer: Establish a new government without corruption hidden under the color of law to govern the things of the land and sea, including human beings.

Jesus Opposed Usury

Interest rates employed within this world of legal fiction is setup by Board members of the Federal Reserve System. This board of men and women has never outright instructed members of the community of Jesus not to render unto God His thing.

I say again, what is God's thing. His thing is a lawful government system that can be established now and here within North America headed by black America—the community of Jesus. As former President Bill Clinton once said, "It's the economy stupid." Yes it is the economy, but a lawful one without usury. Jesus of 2000 years ago was opposed to usury and the Islamic Jesus to return shall be opposed to usury.

The first European banker permitted to experiment with usury, after the age of enlightenment for Europeans, was Sir Richard Hoare. In 1672 Richard established his own bank. Prior to this effort, he sent his early life working as an apprentice for the Goldsmith's Company. This London based company was a part of the trade associations known as the Worshipful Company of the relevant trade or profession. The Worshipful  Company were responsible for the regulation of London, England's trades, controlling, for instance, wages and labour conditions and well as evaluating gold and eventually issuing paper money.[31]

Jesus of the Islamic world who returns is not against lending. He is against usury (compounding interest rates) applied to loans. This corrupt and unjust factor is what devours humanity into debt like a beast preying upon a little lamb. What is compounding interest rates?

> Compound interest arises when interest is added to the principal, so that from that moment on, the interest that has been added also itself earns interest. This addition of interest to the principal is called compounding (i.e. the interest is compounded).
>
> A loan, for example, may have its interest compounded every month: in this case, a loan with $100 initial principal and 1% interest per month would have a balance of $101 at the end of the first month, $102.01 at the end of the second month, and so on." Put another way, the borrower is charged interest on previous interest.[32]

That is to say, America's commercial world is rooted in compound interest rates (usury) passed on to its consumers.

---

[31] The Federal Reserve System: In God We Trust: page 65-66, by Rasheed L. Muhammad.
[32] http://en.wikipedia.org/wiki/Compound_interest

Inside the usurious world of—the "United States" a federal corporation—is where antichrist economic corruption thrives under a color of law, written by white authority. Therefore, it is also here where Jesus, will set down the tyrants and remove them from controlling the peoples treasury and wealth. Maybe to your surprise, the Islamic Jesus is the Christ who returns to free his people from the legal processes of legal fiction.

Legal fiction has destroyed common people's wealth and spending power. Therefore, it cannot stand because it is of the antichrist people or a criminal people as the Holy Quran says.

Gold and Silver in Bible Prophecy

Gold and Silver, as is all of creation, are from God, and given to man for good use, for a useful purpose. (Genesis 1:28, Gen 2:12.) Gold, silver, seed, and flour, were all used as money. (Lev 27:16, 2 Kings 7:1) The vast majority of the time that gold and silver are mentioned in the Bible, it is in reference to the wealth of the kings of Israel or to the wealth of the temple of the Lord. Gold and sliver were used in the workings and furnishings of the ark of the covenant, and the vessels in the temple. Therefore, gold is definitely the approved by God for men to use as money and as a store of wealth.[33]

I took the above statement from an online article written by Jason Hommel. In his article, he discusses the evils of the current fiat monetary systems of the world, and a better understanding of where he thinks we are headed.

Mr. Hommel also suggest one study the economic system that God gave the Israelites in the Hebrew

---

[33] http://www.bibleprophesy.org/goldsilver.htm

Scriptures of the Old Testament, and compare it to what has occurred in America and around the world. As soon as you realize what has happened, economically, you will bear witness how the mind of el Diablo dominates white authority. They seem to love legalizing debt and neither Christian, Jew nor Muslim controls the purse strings of the "United States" a federal corporation, it is controlled by the Synagogue of Satan. To bring this point to modern times, I will simply quote on the following statement made by the Honorable Minister Louis Farrakhan Muhammad: "The thinking of the neo-conservatives is written of in scripture. In the Book of Revelations 2 and 9, it reads: "'I know the blasphemy of those who say they are Jews and are not, but are a synagogue of Satan.'"[34]

In February 2009 Andrew Sullivan wrote he no longer took neo-conservatism seriously because its basic tenet was defense of Israel:

> The closer you examine it, the clearer it is that neo-conservatism, in large part, is simply about enabling the most irredentist elements in Israel and sustaining a permanent war against anyone or any country who disagrees with the Israeli right. That's the conclusion I've been forced to these last few years. And to insist that America adopt exactly the same constant-war-as-survival that Israelis have been slowly forced into... But America is not Israel. And once that distinction is made, much of the neoconservative ideology collapses.

Critics consider neo-conservatism a bellicose and "heroic" ideology opposed to "mercantile" and "bourgeois" virtues and therefore "a variant of anti-economic thought".[78] Political scientist Zeev Sternhell states that "Neo-conservatism has succeeded in convincing the great majority of Americans that

---

[34] http://www.finalcall.com/artman/publish/Minister_Louis_Farrakhan_9/article_6827.shtml

the main questions that concern a society are not economic, and that social questions are really moral questions."[35]

One day soon, Gold shall be restored for a great economic cause [Matthew 2:11] thus making the world a better place. There will be no more currency speculation after the U.S. dollar and its fraudulent financial system crumple.

According the teachings of the Honorable Elijah Muhammad, the new government will restore the Gold Standard. Also, the last prophet of Islam, Mohammed Ibn Abdullah, is quoted as saying:

> Prophet Muhammad (Peace Be Upon Him) of 1,400 years ago warned Muslims against currency speculation and inequality in barter, stating, "...Gold for gold, silver for, silver, but only if it is like for like." The Prophet of Islam warned against defining money according to one standard at the onset of a transaction and then devaluing that standard at a later point in trade. [36]

All this knowledge white authority (Satan) has read and known about centuries ago. Yet, they have rebelled against basic truths. Consequently, their rebellion made a way for Jesus' return very easy.

I recommend reading the book, "Farrakhan: The Jesus Factor", to gain a clear understanding about Jesus' return, as a Muslim, with The Keys (full knowledge) to establish a new government for all people, all races, all children, all colors.

---

35 35

[36] http://www.finalcall.com/artman/publish/article_3921.shtml

Chapter 6
Land of Make Believe and Debt

Debt is merely a promise to pay later for already handed over goods. Therefore credit and debt existed even before coins. Debt is as old as people doing business with people are. However, the enemies of Jesus and his community made a business out of debt to oppress the people through usury.

Today the enemy of freedom invents all forms of debt security instruments. They have yet to mathematically configured out how lend credit at 0% and still earn a profit.[37]

Naturally, debt financing is used to finance a company or government by selling the bonds, notes or mortgages held by the business or corporation. Of course, debt financing is borrowing money to keep ones business doors open. Long term debt financing is typically associated with larger assets such as buildings, equipment, land, and large machinery or using employed legal persons as assets. A city or state cannot function without businesses, corporations, end-users, public transportation, a labor force of legal persons, etc. All of these elements represent tax revenues to run a nation's, towns, cities and business. However, debt financing must be employed properly i.e., without usury.

North America happened to be the last government Europe's international banking apparatus needed to overcome and to mislead the Black and Red nations' into legal fiction or a commercial world. Their objective was experienced during the 1930's when U.S. Congress empowered them to lend paper money to the U.S.

---

[37] See **www.restoremortgages.com**

Treasury Department. The goal was to establish a global federalized bank with juristic authority. This structure is now in place. Right plan only wrong people to deputize plan.

Nevertheless, the central bankers [person] then converted U.S. Congress to think that paper money was more flexible than Gold. The paper money concept, Marco Polo brought back to Europe after exploring ancient China some centuries ago. Okay, Europe borrowed the paper money concept from ancient China's Song and Ming Dynasty that existed mainly from A.D. 960 - 1644. However, paper money did not endure then and it will not endure under white authorities devaluing fiat money world order.[38]

Think about it. How can artificial corporate PERSON print money at a cost of around 4 cents no matter the domination? Then lend the paper money to an entire government at profits into the trillions of dollars. Simply put, this is out-and-out fraud, except in a world of legal fiction.

Furthermore, it is certainly fraud in the eyes of Jesus and any other prophet. It is a fictional practice due to legal procedures written as a law, under white authority, that must be amended as any other law they've written and amended to serve their own ends. To refuse to amend the laws, which enable financial crimes, is the end of white authority. Some economist predicts the U.S. national debt at a 20 trillion dollar death spiral during year 2015.

---

[38] Classical Gold Standard: Fall of the Caucasian Civilization: page 48, by Rasheed L. Muhammad

United States Declared Bankruptcy

White America surrendered its sovereignty to a private corporate group of person[s] [bank] around the 1930's. Then in 1933, her Congressmen, to insure bank legal processes rule over the public, permitted U.S. Gold to be confiscated out of public hands. This plan was executed under Emergency War Powers Act.

> "The 'Bank Holiday' of March 6, 1933 was part and parcel of the Emergency War Powers Act and the actions which followed, and was primarily intended to prevent the continuing and increasing withdrawal of currency and gold from the banks. This, in effect, was the true national emergency of 1933 (but more an emergency for the bankers than the nation).

> Meanwhile, every President of the United States since Franklin Roosevelt has reaffirmed the "national emergency" and issued Executive Orders under 12 USC 95(a), continuing the US Bankruptcy and "reorganization". [Will there be no end to the reorganization?] Today, things are continuing, with enemies being created everywhere -- from Osama Bin Laden to Saddam Hussein, from Enemy Combatants to you or your neighbor next door. It is not a comforting thought. But it's also true."[39]

The irony is every President of the United States since 1933 must reaffirm a "national emergency" to justify continuing its business under bankruptcy and reorganization. And by so doing means, an enemy combatant must be ever lurking and/or must be ever invented. Hence, today, the Muslim has been demonized

---

[39] www.halexandria.org/dward284.htm

into an enemy combatant, not the Indians, Germans, Koreans or Russians like during the 1600's, 1930's, 40's, 50's, 60's, etc., etc. Thus the Bible reads,

[5]"Look at the nations and watch—and be utterly amazed. For I am going to do something in your days that you would not believe, even if you were told. [6]I am raising up the Babylonians, that ruthless and impetuous people, who sweep across the whole earth to seize dwelling places not their own. [7]They are a feared and dreaded people; they are a law to themselves and promote their own honor. [8]Their horses are swifter than leopards, fiercer than wolves at dusk. Their cavalry gallops headlong; their horsemen come from afar. They fly like a vulture swooping to devour; [9]they all come bent on violence. Their hordes advance like a desert wind and gather prisoners like sand. [10]They deride kings and scoff at rulers. They laugh at all fortified cities; they build earthen ramps and capture them. [11]Then they sweep past like the wind and go on-- guilty men, whose own strength is their god." (Habakkuk 1:5-12)

Habakkuk the prophet could not have given a better prophetic picture to make known what white authority would do and has fulfilled during these end times.

Without war, the Central bank—Federal Reserve Bank System [person]—will not stimulate new loans that facilitate the "United States' a federal corporation to borrow money to refinance its existence as an artificial corporate person too. As a result, in 1933, America declared her bankruptcy or reorganization plan to become the "United States' a federal corporation. This corporation and/ or artificial person were <u>berthed</u> through the Federal Reserve Systems commercial enterprise. Like a mother ship, docking into a port, the privately owned central bank [person] of the U.S. converted all things and people into a negotiable instrument for commercial advantages and profits. As you see, under white authority—Diablo's world—war must go on. It is part of the bank [person] business.

I reiterate a "national emergency" has to be ginned up for refinancing the legal fiction written by doctors of law to establish commercial codes and not Jesus' economic philosophy—wealth distribution!

Mark of White Authority

The poor ignorant masses have been inveigled onto the stage of legal fiction under the guise of the social security number system instituted under President Hoover's administration that had replaced President Franklin D. Roosevelt's administration in 1933.

Under the Roosevelt, administration surfaced *The New Deal*. With this deal, all U.S. citizens, in 1936, were required to receive a number or mark of white authority, as the Christians were unaware, [Rev 13: 16-17].

After Roosevelt's era legalized the social security number system (SSN), it became a law under Federal Reserve Provisions. Each SSN represented income tax dollars needed to finance a gigantic bureaucracy—the "United States" a federal corporation and its international private families for lending the money.

A social security number or card, allows a human being to begin living his or her life as a legal person or corporate entity PERSON, yet, without the full benefits given to corporations such as an employer. So once again, what is a person in the world of legal fiction according Uniform Commercial Code 27?

> **"Person"** means an individual, corporation, business trust, estate, trust, partnership, Limited Liability Company, association, joint venture, government, governmental subdivision, agency, or instrumentality, public corporation, or any other legal or commercial entity.[40]

To the private owners of this world's central bank corporation—Federal Reserve Bank, you have done a fine job holding elite Caucasian bloodlines in power while temporarily trumping God's law. However, as prophesied by the Islamic world, Jesus and his community will take from here. I reiterate, you have done a fine job, but "we' will take it from here in the Name of Allah, who came in the Personage of Master W. Fard Muhammad as taught by the Honorable Elijah Muhammad.

For now, white authority governs and rules by land and sea laws of commerce and trade. They have plans to subject all, including the Allah people to get tagged and tracked into a world of legal fiction. Therefore, it's no wonder the Bible revelator [10:2] prophesies of Jesus' return with one foot on land and other foot on sea? *"He was holding a little scroll, which lay open in his hand. He planted his right foot on the sea and his left foot on the land...?"*

You read how Jesus takes the law of God to study and then applies it correctly to establish heaven on earth as

---

[40] http://www.law.cornell.edu/ucc/1/article1.htm#s1-201

a lawful government. After that, white authority shall be outdone. Wealth will be in abundance and no one will pay taxes, as we now know it. But for now, we live under Bank Law.

Chapter 7
Final Call

Mr. Elijah Muhammad delivered the following words in 1973, entitled "A Saviour is born." Here is a powerful excerpt from the lecture, which gives white authority a way into the future of the new rulers of the new government:

> This race of people -- the white race -- was not made to be saved. Some of them will live, though, for a long time, many centuries, those who have accepted Islam. There are many more of them that still await their turn to acknowledge Islam. They are coming into Islam, now, very fast, because they know the day they are living in and the time.
>
> But there will be some that stick around maybe a thousand years. But they can't go beyond the thousand years, even if they have not or if they have believed, they can't go beyond the thousand years.
>
> I won't go into no more of that, but that is true. But a man living here today that can not hardly make it too far over fifty-four years old, he says that's okay with him if he can stick around that long – a thousand years.

In terms of the 1000 years and how it relates to the Christian calendar, MUHAMMAD did go further to clarify the calendar science of what 1000 years mean concerning the end of white authority. He said:

> "This is what is meant by the old passing away and a new coming into existence. There was a new world of the White race that came into a vacuum in our history, from the 9,000th year *[6000 B.C.]* to the 15,000th year *[1914 A.D. or Christian calendar]* of our calendar history, a vacuum made in our past 16,000 years, of 6,000 years, given to the white race to rule.

We are now in the 15,000th year *[year 2012 = year 15098]* of our calendar history of 25,000 years...

The rule of the White race terminates at the 16,000th year *[2914 A.D.]* and that year is the beginning of the Black Nation's rule again, as we ruled before the 9,000th year of Yakub's [Jacob's] making.[41]

Evidence of Black rule before the white race (Adam and Eve) were made is also hidden in Genesis 4: Verse 1: Adam and eve had two children; **Cain and Abel...**Verse 8: **Then Cain slew Abel**, and God cursed him. (So, only Cain, Adam and Eve remained on earth.)...Verse 17: And **Cain knew his wife**; and she conceived, and bare Enoch: **And he builded a city**, and called the city Enoch. (Now, there were only Adam, Eve and Cain on the earth, **where did he find a wife**? and then, he build a city. **He must have been a madman to build a city on his own, and that for three people?** This is enough evidence to prove that there were people before Adam and Eve, and that they were there when Adam was created. [42]

Adam in this biblical case represents the white race or made man. There biblical history hides them under the name Yakub (Jacob). The Ancient Black Nation (first people on earth) were tricked out of power 6,000 years ago by the made-man or race according to [Genesis 25:23] *"The LORD said to her, "Two nations are in your womb; And two peoples will be separated from your body; And one*

---

[41] (Reprinted from "Our Saviour Has Arrived," 1974.)

[42] http://thehiddenverses.blogspot.com/2010/02/were-there-people-on-earth-before-adam.html

people shall be stronger than the other And the older
[black nation] shall serve the younger [white authority]."

The wisest members of Yakub's made race were later called Jews because they were the first Caucasians to obey Musa (Moses), the lawgiver, around 4000 B.C., thus they were able to exit the Caucus Mountains. That was, according to the Original Asiatic Calendar, year 11,000 from year 1 of the 25,000-year cycle—procession of the equinox of our present dispensation of universal time.

> **Precession** It takes to Earth's axis **25,771.5 years** to make one full cycle before beginning a new cycle among the stars, centered on the ecliptic north pole with an angular radius of about 23.3°. [Source]: IAU 2006 Resolution B1, Adoption of the PO3 Precession Theory and Definition of the Ecliptic]

The opening of the Black Nations rule began when the Nation of Islam was founded in the West in 1930. Its wisdom is directly from the teachings of Master W. Fard MUHAMMAD, The Great Mahdi and His servant the Hon. Elijah MUHAMMAD. The civilization FARD came to put down to replace is Yakub's (Jacob's) 6,000 year old civilization. This man Yakub (Jacob) is the biblical father of the white race—the youngest race on our planet and the reason they have acted and ruled like a juvenile among the originals.

Was there a reason Master W. Fard Muhammad, finder of the lost and found members of the Nation of Islam in North America, came during the time she was conquered by Europe's central bankers? YES!

First, and foremost the community of Jesus are members of the once lost Black Nation. Its finder was born in Mecca, Arabia, 1877—the same year America's Supreme Court outlawed Black America's reconstruction era because a deal took place between International BANKERS and the U.S. Congress.

> The end of Reconstruction…With the Compromise of 1877, **Army intervention** in the South ceased and Republican control collapsed…in the South. This was followed by a period that white Southerners labeled Redemption, in which white-dominated state legislatures enacted Jim Crow laws and disfranchised most blacks…through a combination of constitutional amendments and electoral laws…**imposing the system of white supremacy** and second-class citizenship for blacks, known as the age of Jim Crow.[43]

The blear-eyed devils ultimate deal and aim was to keep their army in place to suppress the rise of Black America. Hence, [Holy Quran 20:102] *"The Day the Horn will be blown. And We will gather the criminals, that Day, blue-eyed."* Their worst crime ever committed is the Atlantic slave trade beginning in the Christian year of 1555. So by the year 1931, Master Wallace Fard Muhammad, at age 54, began teaching one of North America's former slave descendants, Elijah Muhammad, face to face for 3.5 years preparing him to find a minister to help in the mission of resurrecting America's victims of slavery. That minister or helper was Louis Gene Walcott, born in 1933, who later was renamed FARRAKHAN in 1965. The year 1933 is also the year Master Wallace. Fard Muhammad began to sign His name as such to express the meaning of One Who had come in the Early Morning Dawn of the New

---

[43] http://en.wikipedia.org/wiki/Reconstruction_era_of_the_United_States

Millennium to lay the base for a New World Order of Peace and Righteousness on the foundation of Truth and Justice; to put down tyrants and to change the world into a Heaven on Earth.

In summary, the factors of the life of Jesus apply to three men and a once lost people i.e., Black America in the "United States" a federal corporation. The three key figures of the Jesus Factor are shown below in black and white.

The final frontier to straighten out is the implementation of a new law that shall govern both the land and the sea setting people free all over the planet earth. Will the final resolution take place through a U.S. court? To reject the Nation of Islam—Black America—in relationship with the life of Jesus and his community is to reject the hereafter. However, you might perceive the Jesus factor, time is not on the side of the world of legal fiction [Matthew 24:22] *"In fact, unless that time of calamity is shortened, not a single person will survive. But it will be shortened for the sake of God's chosen ones."*